GARLANDS

&wreaths

flower circles

GARLANDS
&*wreaths*
flower circles

stunning floral designs for natural displays

BEVERLEY JOLLANDS

LORENZ BOOKS

This edition published by Lorenz Books
an imprint of
Anness Publishing Limited
Hermes House
88-89 Blackfriars Road
London SE1 8HA

This edition distributed in Canada by Raincoast Books
8680 Cambie Street, Vancouver, British Columbia, V6P 6M9

ISBN 0-7548-0140-3

A CIP catalogue record for this book is available from the British Library

Publisher: Joanna Lorenz
Project Editor: Joanne Rippin
Editor: Beverley Jollands
Illustrator: Anna Koska
Designer: Lisa Tai

Previously published as part of the *Gifts from Nature* series

Printed and bound in Singapore

© Anness Publishing Limited 1997, 1999

1 3 5 7 9 10 8 6 4 2
The publishers would like to thank the following project contributors:
Fiona Barnett pp12, 32, 33, 40, 41, 42, 50, 62; Tessa Evelegh pp10, 14, 16, 18, 36, 46, 52, 56; Lucinda Ganderton p58;
Terence Moore pp20, 22, 24, 25, 30, 48; Kally Ellis and Ercole Moroni p26; Katherine Richmond pp56, 60;
Pamela Westland pp38, 39; Dorothy Wood p54;
Photographs by: James Duncan, John Freeman, Debbie Patterson, Polly Wreford.

CONTENTS

INTRODUCTION

Swags, garlands, wreaths and rings take floral decorations beyond vases and bowls and give you the scope to make wonderful large-scale statements when you are decorating your home for a special occasion. They will enhance architectural features of which you are particularly fond, and give a feeling of opulence and generosity in keeping with a festive mood. Don't save these creations only for grand occasions, however. Simply-decorated twig or wicker rings make charming wall ornaments almost anywhere, while a rope of herbs is both beautiful and useful in the kitchen.

Before you begin, think carefully about the scale of your decoration: for example, check that your Christmas wreath will be in proportion to your front door; cut ropes for swags and garlands generously enough to enable them to drape beautifully. If you are making a long swag you may find it easier to construct it in several shorter sections which can be joined afterwards. Dried material, particularly, can be quite stiff, and trying to bend the swag into shape after it is finished may create gaps that are difficult to hide.

For swags and garlands, the amount of material you will need will depend on the length of your finished decoration. For a lavish effect, base your design on something that you can get plenty of: evergreens from your own garden, for instance. Make a lovely thick rope of these, against which the cones, nuts, fruits or flowers which form the highlights of the decoration can be set. Whether you are planning a grand entertainment or are just feeling creative, you'll find inspiration in this collection of enchanting, natural decorations.

SWAGS AND GARLANDS

The sinuous movement of a garland of fresh flowers draped over a doorway or twined about a balustrade gives a truly opulent feel to your decorative schemes, as does a stunning  autumn swag crowning the mantelpiece. Lush ropes of fresh flowers and foliage take time to prepare, but the effort is always worthwhile for a grand occasion such as a wedding or a special party. You can also create

 pretty effects on a less lavish scale with simple strings of dried fruits, nuts and spices, or bunches of fresh herbs. Use dried flowers and foliage to make dramatic swags that will last for months.

PROVENÇAL HERB SWAG

Fix bunches of fresh herbs to a thick plaited (braided) rope, add tiny pots to give the design structure, and then use garlic and colourful chillies as focal points to make a vibrant kitchen decoration full of Provençal flavour, for anyone who loves to cook.

- seagrass string
- scissors
- garden twine
- stub (floral) wires
- fresh sage
- fresh thyme

- fresh oregano
- 2 small flowerpots
- 2 garlic bulbs (heads)
- glue gun (optional)
- large dried red chillies

1 Cut six lengths of seagrass string about three times the length of the hanging. Fold two lengths in half and place them under a length of garden twine. Pass the cut ends over the twine and through the loop to knot the seagrass on to the twine. Repeat with the remaining lengths. Divide the seagrass into three bundles of four lengths and plait (braid) them together.

*I*f you can't find any dried chillies, try drying your own by placing large, fresh chillies in an oven set at a low temperature. When they have darkened and shrivelled, hang the chillies until they feel dry to the touch.

2 Cut another length of seagrass string and bind it around the end of the plait (braid) to finish it. Using stub (floral) wires, bind the herbs into small bundles and tie each one with garden twine. Use the twine to tie them on to the seagrass base, arranging the different herbs evenly down the plait (braid).

3 Wire the flowerpots by passing two stub (floral) wires through the central hole and twisting the ends together.

4 Wire the pots to the base by passing a stub (floral) wire through the wires on the pots and through the plait (braid), then twisting the ends together.

5 Tie garden twine around the garlic bulbs (heads) and tie these to the base. Wire or glue the chillies into position, and fill the pots with more chillies.

FRUIT AND FLOWER SWAG

The visual freshness of this decorative swag makes it especially suitable for a kitchen but, if you made it on a longer base, you could use it equally successfully as a mantelpiece garland or even extend it to adorn the balustrade of a staircase.

- stub (floral) wires
- 4 limes
- 9 lemons
- 4 bunches black grapes
- 4 bunches helenium (sneezeweed)

- 1 bundle tree ivy
- scissors
- straw plait, (braid) about 60 cm (24 in) long
- raffia
- trailing ivy

1 Pass a wire through each of the limes and lemons, just above the base. Leave equal lengths of wire projecting from either side, bend these down and twist together under the base. If the lemons are heavier, pass a second wire through at right angles to the first and twist all four ends together.

Although lemons and limes will survive quite well, the grapes and cut flowers will need regular misting with water to keep them looking fresh.

2 Group the grapes in small clusters and bind with stub (floral) wires, bending the ends of the wire straight down to form a mount. Form 12 small bunches of helenium (sneezeweed) mixed with tree ivy and wire these in the same way.

3 Starting at the bottom of the plait (braid), bind on three wired lemons with raffia. Then bind, in turn, a bunch of flowers and foliage, a lime, some grapes and a second bunch of flowers and foliage.

4 Repeat this sequence, binding the material to the plait (braid) until almost at the top. Secure by wrapping the end of the length of raffia tightly around the top of the swag.

5 Make a bow from raffia and tie to the top of the swag. Trim off any stray wire ends. Entwine the trailing ivy around the top of the swag and the raffia bow.

SPICED FRUIT GARLAND

Raid the storecupboard and scrap box, add garden clippings and dried fruit slices, and you have the ingredients for a delightfully simple garland. It's pretty at any time of year, but its evocative scents and colours make it a lovely alternative to Christmas tinsel.

- stub (floral) wires
- bundles of twigs
- picture framer's wax gilt
- dried bay leaves
- dried pear slices
- fabric scraps
- dried apple slices
- dried orange slices
- small elastic bands
- cinnamon sticks
- gold twine
- beeswax candle ends

1 Wire together bundles of twigs, then gild them by rubbing in picture framer's wax gilt using your finger.

2 Make a loop at one end of a stub (floral) wire. Thread on dried bay leaves, then a dried pear slice. Make a hook at the top.

3 Tie a scrap of coloured fabric to the bottom loop and a scrap of green chiffon at the top, to look like leaves. Make apple-slice bundles by threading on two or three thick apple slices first, then the bay leaves.

4 Wire pairs of thin apple slices by passing a wire through the centre of each and twisting them together at the top. Wire the orange slices in the same way. Use small elastic bands to make bundles of cinnamon sticks.

5 Make a garland to hang from a shelf or at the window, or to drape around the Christmas tree, stringing the decorations on gold twine. The beeswax candle ends are knotted into the garland at intervals.

LAVENDER AND SUNFLOWER GARLAND

Spread a little scented sunshine with this vibrant dried garland. It makes an opulent decoration for the top of a dresser or wardrobe, kitchen cupboards or a mantelpiece, and its fragrance will last for months.

- plastic garland case
- kitchen knife
- dry florist's foam blocks
- scissors
- sunflower heads
- dried curry plant
- dried lavender

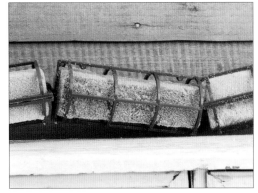

1 The garland base consists of plastic cases. Fill these with florist's foam, cut to fit.

2 Link the cases together and position along a shelf to make the desired length of garland.

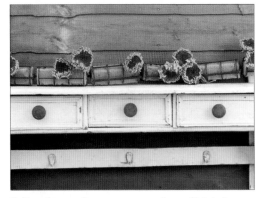

Try to construct this garland in its display position, as the linked garland cases are difficult to move when filled.

3 Cut the sunflower stems to 5 cm (2 in). Insert the sunflowers in groups at intervals along the length of the garland. Add dried curry flowers around the sunflower heads.

4 Trim the lavender stalks to 5 cm (2 in) and add them to fill the remaining spaces along the garland. Work outward from each group of sunflowers, making sure that all the florist's foam is covered.

SPRINGTIME GARLAND

Garlands of fresh flowers make delightful decorations for any celebration. This pretty little hanging of pansies and violas has a woodland feel that can be re-created at any time, because these plants are available for most of the year.

- wire cutters
- chicken wire
- scissors
- black plastic sheeting
- about 2 pansy plants for each 15 cm (6 in) of garland

- about 6 viola plants for each 15 cm (6 in) of garland
- stub (floral) wires
- moss

1 Using wire cutters, cut the chicken wire to the length of the finished garland and three times its width. Bend it into a roll and flatten it slightly.

2 Cut the plastic sheeting into squares large enough to wrap the rootballs of the plants. Unpot each plant and place the rootball in the centre of a square.

3 Gather the plastic around the rootball and fix it by winding a stub (floral) wire around the top, leaving a short length to fix to the garland.

4 Fix the bagged-up plants to the garland using the free end of the wire.

5 Finish off by covering any visible plastic with moss, fixing it with stub (floral) wires bent into a U-shape.

SUMMER TABLE SWAG

A rich, colourful collection of dried flowers has been used to create this summer table swag; combined with fresh fruit and candles, this arrangement is ideal for a summer evening dinner in the garden. You can open the flowers by holding them in steam for a few seconds, to lift the creases from the petals.

- wheat
- dried oregano
- dried *Eucalyptus spiralus*
- dried pink larkspur
- scissors
- florist's reel wire
- rope
- dried peonies
- dried pink roses
- kettle
- glue gun
- selection of candles
- terracotta flowerpots
- green moss
- fresh fruit

1 Separate the stems of the plant material (excluding the peonies and roses), trim them to about 15–20 cm (6–8 in) and make a pile of each variety. Starting with the wheat, bind the materials to the rope in small bunches using florist's reel wire.

2 Continue to cover the rope in this manner, distributing the material evenly along its entire length. Make sure that the garland is really full by allowing some of the material to trail on to the work surface as it is tied to the rope.

3 Choose the ingredients carefully to achieve a good balance of colour and form. Remember that the brighter colours, such as the pink of the larkspur, will stand out more strongly than the darker colours.

4 Steam the roses and peonies to make them as open as possible. Cut the stems from the flower heads and glue them to the swag, spacing them evenly along the whole length. Arrange the candles in pots, placing moss and fruit freely to cover all the fixings.

SUMMER WEDDING SWAG

This pretty, soft combination is ideal for a summer wedding and can be made to any length to fit your chosen location.
It would look very welcoming fixed in an arch above the church door, or you could make a pair to hang on either side. This combination
of materials also works well inside the church: a long version would look very impressive twined around a stone pillar.

- rope
- scissors
- dried nigella
- dried oregano
- dried pink larkspur
- florist's reel wire
- stub (floral) wires
- dried lavender
- dried pink roses
- gauze fabric or ribbon
- glue gun

WINTER VARIATION

This winter version is made in exactly the same way, but it is on a larger scale and has been laid on the floor. A pair of these running down either side of the aisle of the church makes a stunning display. The bow is constructed from chicken wire filled with sphagnum moss, with a thin layer of green moss tied over it with florist's reel wire. Great care needs to be taken with the candles, and it would be wise to do without them unless there is plenty of space.

1 Cut the rope to the required length, allowing extra at each end to make a hanging loop. Trim all the plant stems to about 15 cm (6 in) and make separate piles of each type. Using florist's wire, tie on a small bunch of nigella to cover the loop at one end of the rope.

2 Move along the rope, covering the stems of the nigella with a small bunch of oregano, again fixing it in place with florist's reel wire. Repeat the process by wiring on a small bunch of pink larkspur.

3 Continue binding small bunches of the different materials to the rope in this order, making sure that when the swag is lying on a flat surface there are no gaps along its sides.

4 Make small bunches of the lavender and the roses, tying each bunch in the centre with a stub (floral) wire. Add these almost at right angles to the swag, and twist the ends of each wire together at the back. Tie a bow in the gauze and glue it to one end.

NUT AND CONE GARLAND

This autumnal decoration is simple and quick to make using a glue gun to attach the cones and nuts. If you can't find a ready-made vine ring you could make your own, using vines or twigs cut when green and pliable. Twist them on to a wire base: once dry, the material will hold its shape. Add a red paper bow, lightly sprayed with gold paint, to enhance the warm tones of the nuts.

- glue gun
- fir cones
- ready-made vine or hay ring
- selection of nuts (brazil nuts, walnuts and hazelnuts)

- red paper bow, lightly sprayed with gold paint

As Christmas approaches, you can give the nuts and cones a frosted look with a coat of silver, gold or white spray paint. Spray very lightly, to allow some of the natural colour of the materials to show through.

1 Glue the fir cones on to the vine or hay ring in groups of 4 or 5, leaving a good space between each group. Give an impression of weight to the garland by using the larger fir cones in groups at the bottom and any smaller ones on the sides and top of the ring.

2 Add the nuts, either in groups of a single variety or mixed together. In either case, hide as much of the vine ring underneath as possible. Arrange the nuts more thickly towards the bottom of the ring. Glue the bow in place at the top of the ring.

WINTER FIREPLACE SWAG

This very grand swag uses a dark, rich mixture of materials to create its winter feel. Use blue pine (spruce) while it is still fresh and it will provide a soft base for the other materials. It will slowly dry out, but it will keep for many months in dry conditions. For Christmas you could add dark red ribbons and gold-sprayed cones. Keep the swag well away from an open fire.

- rope
- scissors
- dried red amaranthus
- dried marjoram
- holly oak
- blue spruce
- florist's reel wire
- cones
- dried oranges
- dried chillies
- kutchi fruit
- glue gun
- dried red roses
- dried lavender
- stub (floral) wires
- pliers
- green moss
- mossing (floral) pins (optional)

1 Cut a length of rope for each side of the swag, and make a hanging loop at each end. Trim the amaranthus, marjoram, holly oak and blue spruce and sort into piles. Using florist's reel wire, tie small bunches of each variety in turn to the rope. Work roughly in a zig-zag, making sure that there are no spaces along the bottom edges. Repeat the process for the second rope to match.

2 Fix the remaining materials at intervals along the two lengths of swag wherever they are required to make a balanced, full design. The cones, dried oranges and woody items can be glued in place. Make small bunches of the roses and lavender and bind with stub (floral) wires, using the ends to attach them to the swag. Fill any small spaces with moss, pinning or gluing it in place as you prefer.

WINTER WEDDING GARLAND

It takes time and patience to put together a blue spruce garland like this one – but it is certainly worth the effort.
Intended to be held by two bridesmaids or page boys, it is full of natural movement and colour. All the materials are wired on as
densely as possible, in clusters, to give the piece a feeling of unabashed opulence.

- string or garden twine
- scissors
- florist's reel wire
- blue spruce
- stub (floral) wire
- pine cones (natural and gold-sprayed)
- gloriosa
- walnuts
- gloxinia
- guelder rose (European cranberry) berries
- gold-sprayed cardoon
- ribbon

1 Cut the string to approximately 90 cm (36 in) and make a small loop at either end. Attach the florist's reel wire just below one of the loops. Prepare small sprigs of blue spruce and attach the first one by binding the wire twice around the base.

2 Stagger the subsequent pieces of blue spruce along the string, rotating the body of the garland as you go. Bind in each piece individually with the florist's reel wire. Continue until you reach the other end of the string. Tie off the wire.

3 Wire each pine cone by passing a stub (floral) wire around the prongs of the lower part of the cone and twisting the two ends together. Attach the cones in groups of three at regular intervals along the garland.

4 Wire three gloriosa heads together. Arrange these triple heads in groups of three, by pushing the wires through the body of the garland and bending them back around the garland to secure them.

5 Continue to group clusters of flowers, berries and wired nuts at intervals along the garland until it is generously covered. Thread a length of ribbon through the string loop at each end, to make a carrying loop, and finish with a bow.

RINGS AND TABLE DECORATIONS

Flower-filled rings make a perfect decoration for a table: they won't obstruct the diners' view of each other, they can't be knocked over, and they are always a conversation-piece. If you are dining by candlelight, sit the candles in the centre or attach some small pots to the ring before adding the flowers so that you can tuck the candles in afterwards. For winter

decorations, use aromatic spices and fruit with fresh or dried foliage. Stunning effects can be created by contrasting the formality of the ring with arrangements that spill out in all directions.

SUNFLOWER RING EXTRAVAGANZA

This flamboyant garland celebrates the strong colour and echoes the dramatic circular shape of sunflowers.
Tie the flowers as low down their stems as you can to avoid a flat, cramped look – you should be able to push your fingers easily
around the flowers. It's important to keep a good balance of colour and shape, so stand back often and take a good look.

- metal ring covered with hay or moss
- stub (floral) wires
- selection of dried flowers such as alchemilla, amaranthus, blue larkspur, carthamus, eucalyptus, nigella, sunflowers and twigs
- scissors
- florist's reel wire
- glue gun
- moss (optional)

1 Fix a stub (floral) wire to the hay ring, to create a hanging loop. Bend the wire into a U-shape, then push the two ends through the ring from the back.

2 Check that the loop made by the wire is large enough, and pull or push the wire through the hay ring to adjust the size of the loop as necessary.

3 Twist the ends of the wire together and tuck them neatly into the hay. You may prefer to decide which way up to hang the garland after you have decorated it, and add the wire loop at that point.

4 Separate the flowers into bunches and trim each stem to about 20 cm (8 in). Lay the flowers in the position you want and wind florist's reel wire round the ring to hold the stems tightly in place. Large-headed flowers can be glued into place at the end. Cut the stems short before applying the glue. Fill any spaces by gluing on small bunches of flowers or hanks of moss.

FRESH ROSE VALENTINE RING

While this delightful floral circlet could be used at any time of the year, the impact created by the massed red roses makes it particularly appropriate to Valentine's Day. It can be used as a table decoration for a romantic dinner.

- 15 cm (6 in) diameter florist's foam ring
- dark green ivy leaves

- stub (floral) wires
- wire cutters
- bun moss
- 20 dark red roses
- scissors

1 Soak the foam ring in water. Push individual, medium-sized ivy leaves into the foam to create an outline around the ring. Make U-shapes with the stub (floral) wires and pin on small pieces of bun moss between the ivy.

2 Cut the rose stems to about 4 cm (1½ in) long and push them into the foam until the ring is evenly covered. Gently ease the ivy leaves up, so that they are still visible between the rose heads. Keep the ring damp.

CINNAMON AND ORANGE RING

The warm colours and spicy smell of this small ring make it perfect for the wall of a kitchen. The display is not complicated to make but requires nimble fingers: the pieces of cinnamon have to be tightly packed together to achieve the right effect. To reinforce the foam, you could glue it to a piece of stiff cardboard cut to the same outline before starting to assemble the ring.

- glue gun
- 5 dried oranges
- 13 cm (5 in)

- diameter florist's dry foam ring
- 20 cinnamon sticks

1 Apply glue to the bases of the dried oranges and fix them to the dry foam ring, equally spaced around it. Break the cinnamon sticks into 2–4 cm (³⁄₄–1¹⁄₂ in) pieces.

2 Apply glue to the bottom of the pieces of cinnamon and push them into the foam between the dried oranges, keeping them close together to achieve a massed effect.

3 Glue a line of cinnamon pieces around both the inside and outside edges of the ring to cover the foam completely.

SUMMER CANDLE RING

This striking chandelier is designed to hang fairly low over a table, so no flowers have been added to the base.
If you wish to hang it higher, turn the display over so that it sits on the rims of the pots, and cover the base with flowers.
When the base is finished, tie the ropes to the hanging points before moving it, so you can avoid resting it the right way up again
and crushing the flowers underneath.

- glue gun
- florist's dry foam
- 30 cm (12 in) wire ring frame
- 4 terracotta flowerpots
- sphagnum moss
- florist's reel wire
- stub (floral) wires
- dried blue and pink larkspur
- dried pink roses
- dried *Achillea ptarmica*
- scissors
- dried peonies
- mossing (floral) pins
- dark green moss
- 4 hanging ropes
- 4 candles

1 Glue a small block of florist's dry foam under the ring frame and to the base of a terracotta pot, making sure that at least one of the wires is lying across the foam. Fix the four pots equally spaced round the ring.

2 When the glue has set, wrap sphagnum moss around the ring, holding it in place with florist's reel wire. The layer needs to be about 2.5 cm (1 in) thick. Check that the foam base and the area around the pots is well covered.

3 Push both ends of a stub (floral) wire through the ring, between two pots on the inner edge. Make sure that it crosses the wire frame under the moss. Twist the ends together and tuck them back into the moss. Repeat between each pair of pots.

4 Make centre-wired bunches of the larkspur, roses and *Achillea ptarmica* and push the tails of the wires into the moss frame, angling the material from the inside of the frame to the outside. Fix the materials in the same order in each quarter of the ring.

5 Cut the stems off the peonies and glue the heads into place. Use mossing (floral) pins to attach the green moss to the ring, filling any spaces between the flowers. Attach the hanging ropes to the wire loops, then fit the candles into the pots, packing them with foam and moss.

ADVENT CANDLE RING

An Advent candle ring makes a pretty Christmas centrepiece. This one – decorated with glossy tree ivy, delicate Cape gooseberries, dried citrus fruit slices and bundles of cinnamon sticks – is not only a delight to the eye but also contributes a rich, seasonal aroma.

- florist's foam
- kitchen knife
- florist's ring basket
- 4 church candles
- green moss
- dried orange slices

- stub (floral) wires
- secateurs (pruners)
- cinnamon sticks
- gold twine
- tree ivy
- Cape gooseberries

1 Soak the florist's foam and cut it to fit the ring basket. Position the candles in the foam.

2 Cover the florist's foam with green moss, pushing it well down at the sides of the basket.

3 Wire the orange slices by passing a stub (floral) wire through each slice, then twisting the ends together at the outside edge.

4 Wire the cinnamon sticks into bundles, tie them with gold twine, then pass a wire through the string to fix them. Wire the tree ivy leaves into bunches.

5 Position the ivy leaves in the ring. Decorate by fixing in the orange slices and cinnamon sticks and placing the Cape gooseberries on top of the candle ring at intervals.

MISTLETOE RING

*A symbol of romance and Christmas frivolities,
mistletoe is combined with other evergreens and gilded seed heads
in a wayward wreath that is at once elegant and casual.*

- wheat
- garden twine
- scissors
- linseed (flaxseed)
- gold spray paint
- artificial Christmas roses
- evergreens: cypress, ivy,

mistletoe and eucalyptus
- 30 cm (12 in) stem ring
- stub (floral) wires
- wire cutters
- 1.5 m (1½ yd) shiny ribbon,
  7.5 cm (3 in) wide

1 Gather the wheat stalks into bunches of three or four and bind the stems. Bind the linseed (flaxseed) into bunches of uneven lengths, to give the design its wispy outline. Lightly spray the wheat, linseed (flaxseed), Christmas roses and a few evergreens with gold paint.

2 Secure the bunches to the ring with half a stub (floral) wire bent to make a U-shaped staple. Continue all around the ring, so that the heads of each bunch cover the stems and staples of the one before. Push the roses into the ring at irregular intervals. Tie two ribbon bows and fix them to the wreath with stub (floral) wire staples.

JUNIPER RING

The contrasting characteristics of matt, spiky juniper branches and golden, glowing quinces combine to compose a striking decoration that could hang on a door or a wall. Cypress or yew would be good alternatives for the evergreen ring.

- scissors
- juniper
- garden twine
- 25 cm (10 in) wire ring frame
- heavy-gauge garden wire

- wire cutters
- small quinces
- stub (floral) wires
- florist's reel wire

1 Cut the juniper stems to about 20 cm (8 in) long and gather them into bunches of three, four or five, depending on thickness. Tie the twine to the ring frame and bind on the bunches so that the tips of one cover the stems of the next. Continue until the frame is covered. Measure the heavy-gauge wire against the inside of the evergreen ring and, allowing for a short overlap, cut it to size.

2 Thread the quinces on to the wire and push the two ends into the first and last fruits to be threaded. If this will not hold, join the two fruits together at the back with a stub (floral) wire. Bind the evergreen and the fruit rings together with florist's reel wire, and make a loop for hanging the ring.

TEXTURED FOLIAGE RING

This ring mixes air-dried foliage with leaves preserved with glycerine to create a feast of textures and subtle colours that succeeds without the enhancement of flowers. It makes a wonderful autumn wall decoration. Alternatively, if it can be protected from the weather, it could hang on the front door.

- scissors
- 10 stems dried green honesty
- 5 branches glycerine-preserved beech leaves
- 60 cm (24 in) length dried hop vine
- 5 branches glycerine-preserved adiantum
- 30 cm (12 in) diameter wicker wreath ring
- garden twine

1 Cut all the foliage stems to about 13 cm (5 in) long. You will need 21 lengths of each type of foliage to cover your ring. Start by securely tying a group of three stems of honesty to the wicker ring with the end of the garden twine.

2 Making sure it slightly overlaps the honesty, bind on a group of three glycerined beech stems with the same continuous length of twine. Repeat with three stems of hops, followed by three stems of glycerined adiantum. Continue binding materials to the ring in the same sequence until it is completely covered.

3 Cut off any untidy stems and adjust the materials, if necessary, to achieve the best effect. Finally, tie off the twine in a discreet knot at the back of the ring.

HERBAL TABLE DECORATION

In this original table decoration, a wreath of white dill, softly lit with night-lights (tea-lights), is set around a group of separate terracotta pots, each containing a different herb. Use pots of various sizes within the ring to give height and interest to the arrangement.

- 6 night-lights (tea-lights)
- 30 cm (12 in) florist's foam ring
- 2 blocks florist's foam
- 4 terracotta pots
- cellophane (plastic wrap)
- scissors
- white dill
- rosemary
- mint
- marjoram
- guelder rose (European cranberry) berries

1 Press the night-lights (tea-lights) into the soaked florist's foam ring, spaced equally. Soak the blocks of florist's foam and line the terracotta pots with cellophane (plastic wrap). Cut the florist's foam to size and fit it firmly into the pots.

2 Mass the white dill around the foam ring between the night-lights (tea-lights). Then mass the pots with selected herbs and foliage: for the best effect, fill each pot with one type of herb only. Place the ring in position and arrange the pots within it.

This display can be dismantled and the parts used separately to good effect in different situations. The individual terracotta pots of herbs can even be dried to extend their usefulness. Never leave burning candles unattended.

WEDDING TABLE CIRCLE

A table set for a celebratory lunch doesn't usually have much room to spare on it. In this instance, space has been found for the wine cooler within a sumptuous, textural display of gold, yellow and white flowers with green and grey foliage. The silver is enhanced by the beauty of the decoration and, in turn, its highly polished surface reflects the flowers to increase their impact.

- 40 cm (16 in) diameter florist's foam ring
- scissors
- 12 stems *Senecio laxifolius*
- 15 stems elaeagnus
- 3 groups of 2 chestnuts
- stub (floral) wires
- thick gloves
- wire cutters
- 18 stems yellow roses
- 10 stems cream *Eustoma grandiflorum*
- 10 stems solidago
- 10 stems flowering fennel

1 Soak the foam ring in water. Cut the senecio to a stem length of 14 cm (5½ in) and distribute evenly around the ring, pushing the stems into the foam, to create an even foliage outline. Leave the centre of the ring clear.

2 Cut the elaeagnus stems to a length of 14 cm (5½ in) and distribute evenly throughout the senecio to reinforce the foliage outline, still leaving the centre of the foam ring clear to accommodate the wine cooler.

3 Wearing heavy-duty gloves to protect your hands, push stub (floral) wires through the three chestnut groups, twist the ends together and trim to about 6 cm (2¼ in). Position them at three equidistant points around the ring and push in the wires.

4 Cut the rose stems to about 14 cm (5½ in) and arrange them in staggered groups of three at six points around the ring, equal distances apart, pushing the stems firmly into the foam.

5 Cut stems of single eustoma flower heads 12 cm (4¾ in) long. Arrange the stems evenly in the foam. Cut the stems of solidago to about 14 cm (5½ in) long and distribute throughout. Finally, cut the stems of fennel to about 12 cm (4¾ in) long and add evenly through the display.

HEARTS AND WREATHS

*C*ircles and hearts make charming country-style wall decorations and are a wonderful way to use featherlight dried flowers with their fragile petals and subtle colours. Simplicity is the key to these designs, in which just a few elements are put together to stunning effect. Such light-hearted, informal ornaments look good hung casually from a hook on the kitchen dresser. Use the same light touch for

lovely fresh arrangements: a few ivy stems trailing around a twiggy circlet will make a delicate, original Christmas wreath, while a fresh lavender heart is a restrained yet sensational token of love.

FRESH LAVENDER HEART

There can be little more romantic than a heart made entirely of fresh lavender. Make one for a special occasion, then let it dry naturally as an everlasting souvenir. This uses a lot of lavender, so make sure that you have access to plenty before you begin.

- 120 large stems lavender
- secateurs (pruning shears) or scissors
- florist's reel wire
- garden wire
- florist's tape (stem-wrap tape)
- green raffia

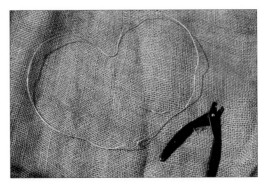

1 Cut the lavender stems to about 2.5 cm (1 in) and make up bunches of about six heads each, firmly securing them with lengths of fine florist's reel wire.

2 Make a hook at each end of a piece of garden wire about 112 cm (44 in) long. Link to make a circle, then make a dip at the top edge and bend into a heart shape.

This amount of fresh lavender will make a heart measuring about 30 cm (12 in) across. If you are not able to find so much fresh lavender use a smaller wire base.

3 Using florist's tape (stem-wrap tape), bind the first bunch of lavender to the bottom of the wire heart. Bind on the next bunch a little further up the wire. Continue until you reach the centre top, then start again at the bottom and work up the other side.

4 Make a small bunch of lavender and secure with wire. Tie with green raffia. Place at the bottom of the front of the wreath and bend the stalks to the back. Pass the raffia to the back to catch the stems and then secure at the front and tie the ends in a bow.

HEART AND FLOWERS

A heart-shaped dried flower decoration with a real feel of the country. The construction of the heart couldn't be simpler, and it will last a long time provided you don't hang it in direct sunlight. This is a lovely way to preserve the best of summer's harvest of roses.

- 4 long stub (floral) wires
- wire cutters
- florist's tape (stem-wrap tape) (optional)
- florist's reel wire
- hay
- scissors
- dark green florist's spray paint
- glue gun or all-purpose glue
- wide red ribbon
- narrow gold ribbon
- large and small dried red roses
- dried hydrangeas

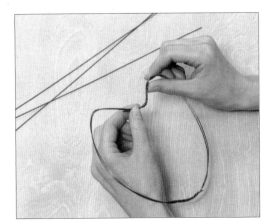

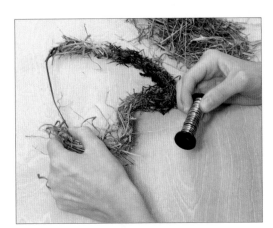

1 Form two pairs of stub (floral) wires into a heart shape. The double thickness of the wire gives the arrangement better support. Twist the ends of the wires together at the top and bottom of the heart shape, and cover the joins with florist's tape (stem-wrap tape) if you wish.

2 Using florist's reel wire, bind hay all round the heart to create a firm frame about twice the thickness of a pencil. Work round the heart at least twice with the wire, to tie in the loose ends of hay. Spray the whole frame dark green.

3 Glue the end of the red ribbon to the bottom of the heart and wrap it round the frame. Repeat with the gold ribbon. Tie a bow at the top with a length of gold ribbon. Cut the stems off the roses and separate the hydrangeas into florets. Glue the large rose heads near the centre and surround them with hydrangeas. Put the smaller rose heads along the top.

EASTER WREATH

Easter is a time of hope and regeneration, and this bright Easter wreath visually captures these feelings. The vibrant colours of the flowers, arranged to look as though they are still growing, give the wreath a fresh, natural glow.

- 30 cm (12 in) diameter florist's foam ring
- elaeagnus foliage
- scissors
- 5 polyanthus plants
- 8 pieces of bark
- stub (floral) wires
- 70 daffodils
- 2 enamel spoons
- natural raffia
- 3 blown eggs

1 Soak the foam ring in water and arrange an even covering of elaeagnus stems, about 7.5 cm (3 in) long, in the foam. At five equidistant positions, add groups of three polyanthus leaves.

2 Wire each piece of bark by bending a stub (floral) wire around the middle and twisting for a tight grip. Position the pieces of bark equidistantly around the ring, using the wires.

3 Arrange the polyanthus flowers in groups of single colours. Leave a gap for the eggs and spoons. Cut the daffodils to a stem length of about 7.5 cm (3 in) and arrange them between the polyanthus, pushing their stems carefully into the foam.

4 Wire the enamel spoons. Position them in the gap, in a cross. Wrap raffia around the blown eggs, then wire them carefully. Arrange the remaining polyanthus flowers and daffodils around the eggs and crossed spoons.

HEART OF WHEAT

Fashion a heart at harvest time, when wheat is plentiful, for a delightful decoration that would look good adorning a wall or a dresser at any time of the year. Despite its delicate feathery looks, this heart is quite robust and should last many years.

- scissors
- heavy-duty garden wire
- florist's tape (stem-wrap tape)
- florist's reel wire
- large bunch of wheat

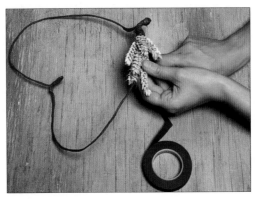

1 Cut three long lengths of heavy-gauge wire and bend them into a heart shape. Twist the ends together at the bottom. Use florist's tape (stem-wrap tape) to bind the wire heart shape.

2 Using florist's wire, make up enough small bundles of wheat ears to cover the wire heart shape densely. Leave a short length of wire at each end for fixing to the heart shape.

3 Starting at the bottom of the wire shape, tape the first bundle of wheat ears to the heart.

4 Place the second bundle further up the heart shape behind the first, and tape it in position. Continue until the whole heart is covered.

5 For the bottom, wire together about six bunches of wheat ears, twist the wires together and wire them to the heart, finishing off with florist's tape (stem-wrap tape) to neaten.

DRIED FLOWER STAR WREATH

In the spring the new, straight growth of woodland trees and shrubs is ideal for collecting and making into a wreath.
Both the colour and shape of this one are novel and fresh, in keeping with the new season.

- 36 thin twigs, about 60 cm (24 in) long
- scissors
- matt acrylic paint in mid-blue
- paintbrush
- florist's reel wire
- 3 m (3 yd) blue and white check
- ribbon, 2 cm (¾ in) wide
- 6 dried pink roses
- selection of dried flowers and plant material in pink, purple and blue
- all-purpose glue
- small, variegated ivy leaves

*A*t Christmas time you could take off the dried flowers, spray the wreath gold and decorate it with tiny fir cones, holly and other festive material.

1 Select the straightest sections of the twigs and trim off the ends to make them about 45 cm (18 in) long. Paint each stick with matt blue acrylic paint and allow to dry.

2 Wire together two bundles of six sticks; add a third bundle to complete a triangle. Weave in three more bundles to make a six-pointed star and wire the points.

3 Wind the ribbon around the central hexagon and tie at the back. Decorate with the rose heads and small sprigs of the other plants, gluing them in place. Stick several ivy leaves at each corner of the hexagon.

4 Wrap a short piece of ribbon around five points of the star and tie at the back. On the sixth point use a longer piece of ribbon and tie the ends into a loop for hanging the wreath.

TWIGGY HEART

Welcome seasonal guests with a door wreath that's charming in its simplicity. Just bend a few twigs into a heart shape and adorn it with variegated ivy, glowing berries and a pure white rose.

- secateurs (pruning shears)
- pliable woody stems, such as buddleia
- florist's reel wire
- seagrass string
- variegated

- trailing ivy
- red berries
- tree ivy
- picture framer's wax gilt (optional)
- white rose
- gold twine

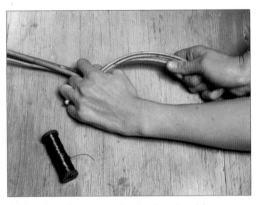

1 Using secateurs (pruning shears), cut six lengths of pliable twigs about 70 cm (28 in) long. Divide into two groups of three and wire together at one end. Cross the two wired ends over and wire them together.

2 Holding the crossed, wired ends with one hand, ease one bundle round and down very gently, so the twigs don't snap. Repeat with the other side, to form a heart shape. Wire the bottom of the heart.

3 Cover the wiring by binding it with seagrass string at top and bottom and make a hanging loop at the top.

4 Entwine strands of trailing ivy delicately around the heart shape.

5 Add berries. Make a posy of tree-ivy leaves (gilded, if you like) and a white rose. Tie with gold twine and wire to the top of the heart.

DRIED LAVENDER WREATH

Lavender has been widely cultivated over centuries for the perfume of its purple flowers, and this wreath will fill any room in which it hangs with the rich scent of summer.

- seagrass rope or coarse string
- 12 in (30 cm) diameter

- twig wreath
- dried lavender stems

1 Tie one end of the natural seagrass rope securely to the wreath. Gather the lavender stems into small bunches.

2 Hold a bunch of lavender across the wreath with the flowers pointing outwards. Wind the rope around the stalks, then over the wreath.

3 Place a second bunch of lavender to the right of the first bunch with the flowers pointing inwards, and wrap the rope once or twice around the stalks. The next bunch goes to the right of the second, with the flowers pointing away from the wreath.

4 Continue to spiral-bind small bunches in the same way, making sure that the twig wreath is concealed. When the ring is completely covered, tie off the end of the rope securely and finish off with a loop for hanging.

FRESH HERBAL WREATH

This scented ring looks fresh and pretty hanging in the kitchen. If you wish, you can include some culinary herbs in your design so that in addition to being decorative, it will act as a dried herb store, and you can snip pieces off the ring as you need them.

- glue gun
- florist's reel wire
- 25 cm (10 in) diameter twig ring
- small bunches of fresh herbs: golden sage, chamomile, lavender, santolina and scented geranium
- scissors
- 2 m (2 yd) co-ordinating ribbon, 2 cm (¾ in) wide

1 Use the glue gun or florist's reel wire to attach a good covering of golden sage and chamomile leaves to the twig ring.

2 Make up small bunches of lavender and santolina, then bind them on to the twig ring with lengths of florist's reel wire. Choose the point where you want to attach the ribbon, and put three medium-sized scented geranium leaves here to act as a backing for the bow. Make double loops and streamers with the ribbon, bind them together with wire and glue or wire them on to the ring.

HERBAL CHRISTMAS WREATH

This unusual wreath incorporates traditional Christmas elements such as holly and glints of gold in a country-style arrangement of dried herbs and wheat. The fresh evergreens will dry on the wreath and continue to look attractive throughout the festive season.

- fresh holly
- 2 sprays fresh conifer
- scissors
- glue gun
- 23 cm (9 in) diameter twisted wicker ring
- gold spray paint
- 5 cm (2 in) terracotta pot
- broken pieces of terracotta pots
- 7 ears of wheat
- dried sage
- dried oregano
- florist's reel wire
- 3 dried orange slices

1 Attach sprigs of the holly and conifer to the ring using the glue gun. Cover about half the ring. Spray a little gold paint on to the pot, pieces of pot, the wheat and the sage.

2 Glue the pot and terracotta pieces to the ring. Add the ears of wheat. Make small bunches of sage and tuck these among the pieces of broken pot. Make a chunky bunch of the dried oregano, wiring it together. Glue into the main pot in the centre of the design. Cut the orange slices into quarters and glue into the arrangement.

CLEMENTINE WREATH

This festive Christmas wreath is full of bold contrasts of colour and shape. It has a citrus smell, but could be made even more aromatic by using bay leaves and other herbs instead of ivy. It will make a spectacular table decoration with one or more candles in the centre.

- stub (floral) wires
- 27 clementines
- wire cutters
- 30 cm (12 in) diameter florist's
- foam ring
- scissors
- pyracanthus berries and foliage
- ivy leaves

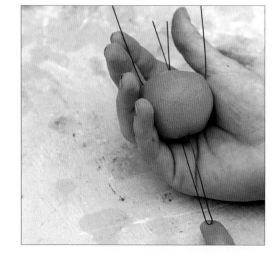

1 Push a stub (floral) wire through the base of each clementine and bend the ends down. Bend another wire into a U-shape and push the ends right through the middle of the fruit so that the bend in the wire is flush with the top. Trim the wires to about 4 cm (1½ in).

2 Soak the florist's foam ring in water. Arrange the wired clementines in a tight circle on the top of the foam ring by pushing their four projecting wire legs into the foam. Form a second ring of clementines within the first ring.

3 Cut the pyracanthus into small stems of berry clusters and foliage about 6 cm (2¼ in) long. Push the stems into the outer side of the foam ring and between the two rings of clementines, distributing them evenly.

4 Cut the ivy leaves into individual stems about 7 cm (2¾ in) in length. Push the stems of the individual leaves into the foam ring, positioning a leaf between each clementine.

INDEX